The MAILBOX®

Ready for September & October

T5-CVG-772

Practical and Fun Activities for Timely Themes

- [ ] **Welcome to Preschool**
- [ ] **All About Me**
- [ ] **Fall Leaves**
- [ ] **Apples**
- [ ] **Fire Safety**
- [ ] **Pumpkins**
- [ ] **Bats**
- [ ] **Spiders**

Managing Editor: Kimberly Ann Brugger

Editorial Team: Becky S. Andrews, Diane Badden, Janet Boyce, Tricia Kylene Brown, Kimberley Bruck, Karen A. Brudnak, Pam Crane, Chris Curry, Roxanne LaBell Dearman, David Drews, Brenda Fay, Deborah Garmon, Tazmen Fisher Hansen, Marsha Heim, Lori Z. Henry, Cynthia Holcomb, Suzanne Moore, Tina Petersen, Mark Rainey, Chelsea Reid, Greg D. Rieves, Mary Robles, Rebecca Saunders, Pam B. Szeliga, Darlene Butler Taig, Donna K. Teal, Sharon M. Tresino, Zane Williard

www.themailbox.com

©2014 The Mailbox® Books
All rights reserved.
ISBN 978-1-61276-434-4

Printed in The United States
10 9 8 7 6 5 4 3 2 1

HPS252656

Table of Contents

What's Inside

Group Time

Centers

Brand-new ideas!

Just what you need to be ready for

September and October!

Songs & Such

Arts & Crafts

Patterns

Tear-Out Teaching Tools

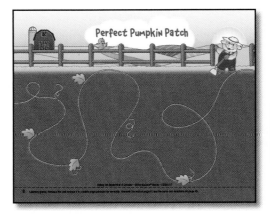

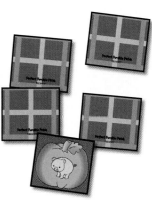

Group Time

Janet!

What Is Your Name?

Getting acquainted with classmates

Help students get to know each other's names with this fun activity. Have students sit in a circle. Then choose a child and encourage her to say her name. Prompt the child to walk around the circle tapping each classmate lightly as you lead students in saying, "We're all different—not the same. We want to learn everyone's name!" When the chant is finished, have the last child tapped say her name. Then the two youngsters switch places, and the game begins again.

Tricia Kylene Brown
Bowling Green, KY

School Bus Sing-Along!

Introducing number names, counting

Arrange several chairs so they resemble the seating on a bus. To begin, hold up a number card and say the name of the number. Have students count out loud as you choose that number of children and encourage them to sit on the bus. Give one child a paper plate steering wheel. Then lead youngsters in a verse of "The Wheels on the Bus" while the driver pretends to drive. Repeat the activity so that every child gets a chance to be on the bus.

Tricia Kylene Brown

There he is!

Where's Walter?

Positional words

Help little ones get comfortable with their classroom! Place a stuffed toy animal in the room before youngsters arrive for the day. During circle time, say, "I wonder where Walter is. Walter is my [type of animal] friend." Have students scan the room for Walter. When a child sees the toy, say, "Oh, there he is!" Then prompt a youngster to use positional words to explain the location. Next, make up a story about what Walter might be doing in that area. For example, say, "Walter is next to the bookcase in the reading area. He must have been looking at one of his favorite books!" Continue this activity each day as desired.

Tricia Kylene Brown
Bowling Green, KY

Crunch!

Sequencing a story

To prepare for this simple pocket chart activity, color and cut out a copy of the apple sequencing cards on page 16 and place them in your pocket chart arranged correctly as shown. Tell students a simple story about a hungry mouse as you point to each card, explaining how the mouse saw a shiny apple, took one bite, took another bite, took a final bite, and then was finished with the apple. As you tell the story, have youngsters make a crunching noise for each appropriate card. Next, switch the locations of two of the cards. Ask, "Does the story make sense now?" Encourage youngsters to explain. Repeat the process several times. When little ones are comfortable, scramble all the cards and help students arrange the story in the correct order.

Mary Robles
Ardenwald Elementary
Milwaukie, OR

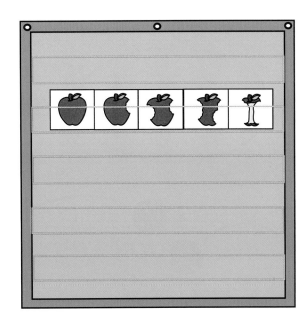

Group Time

Apple, Apple, Worm
Participating in a group game

Here's an apple-themed twist on the traditional game Duck, Duck, Goose! Help youngsters sit in a circle. Then encourage a child to walk around the circle, lightly tapping each child on the head and saying "apple" for each tap. When a child touches a head and says "worm," encourage the youngster who was tapped to stand. Then prompt both children to wiggle enthusiastically while the seated youngsters say, "Wiggle worms, wiggle worms!" The original child sits down, and the child who was tapped becomes the tapper.

Roxanne LaBell Dearman
NC Early Intervention Program for Children Who Are Deaf or
    Hard of Hearing
Charlotte, NC

Alligator!

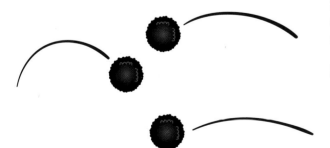

Johnny Appleseed Toss
Recognizing beginning sounds

Seat youngsters in a circle and give each child five black pom-poms (apple seeds). Tell students that they're going to pretend to be Johnny Appleseed. Explain that Johnny Appleseed planted apple seeds wherever he went. Then say a word. If the word begins with /a/, have a child toss an apple seed into the middle of the circle. If it doesn't begin with /a/, the child continues to hold his seeds. Continue until all five seeds are used. Then have each child pick up five seeds for another round.

Roxanne LaBell Dearman

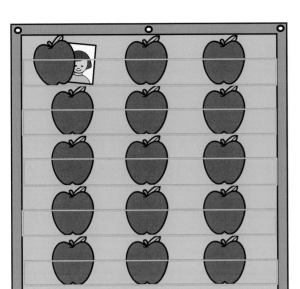

Pick One!

Naming classmates

To prepare for this get-acquainted activity, make a class supply of apple cutouts (pattern on page 45) and place them in your pocket chart. Put a photo of a different student behind each apple. Then gather youngsters around the pocket chart. Call on a child and say, "Pick an apple off the tree. Tell me, tell me who you see!" Then prompt the child to remove an apple. Have her identify her classmate, with help as needed. Then repeat the process until all the apples have been picked.

Tricia Kylene Brown
Bowling Green, KY

All About Me!

Speaking

Youngsters tell about themselves with this chant and activity. Seat students in a circle and then prompt them to clap their hands (or do a simple pattern clapping their hands and patting their legs) as you say, "How do you do? How do you do? Tell me something about you!" Gesture to a child and encourage him to say something about himself, such as his hair color, his name, or whether he has brothers or sisters. Continue the game for several rounds.

Tricia Kylene Brown

I have two sisters!

Group Time

My Favorite Things!

Speaking to express a preference

Put name cards (or name sticks) in a container. To play, lead students in singing the song shown and then draw a card. Ask the child to name a favorite food, color, or toy, prompting him to answer in a complete sentence. Encourage him to take a bow. Then repeat the process with each remaining youngster or break up this activity into a few sessions throughout the day.

(sung to the tune of "Clementine")

What's your favorite, what's your favorite,
What's your favorite? Tell me now.
I would like to know about you.
Tell me and then take a bow.

Tricia Kylene Brown
Bowling Green, KY

My Favorite Food is pizza!

Into the Pile!

Recognizing colors

Get a supply of die-cut leaves (or use cutout copies of the leaf pattern on page 17) in several different colors and give one leaf to each child. Encourage youngsters to stand in a circle. Recite the rhyme shown, encouraging students with leaves of the color named to float and twirl about until they seat themselves in the middle of the circle. Check to make sure all the students in the middle have the appropriate leaf color. Then have them rejoin the circle. Continue with other leaf colors.

Autumn leaves are falling,
Gliding all around.
Here come some [red] ones,
Floating to the ground.

Roxanne LaBell Dearman
NC Early Intervention Program for Children Who Are Deaf or
    Hard of Hearing
Charlotte, NC

Leaves Fall Down!

Identifying shapes

Conceal within a pack of shape cards several cards that show fall leaves. Hold up the cards one at a time, encouraging youngsters to name the shapes. When a leaf card is revealed say, "Rake the leaves!" and encourage students to jump up and pretend to rake leaves. After several seconds of raking, have little ones sit back down and resume the activity.

My Very Own Leaf

Recognizing one's name, following directions

Cut out copies of the leaf pattern on page 17 and label each leaf with a student name. Then scatter the leaves in the middle of your circle-time area so that the names are visible. Say, "If you're wearing green, go and find your leaf." Then help the appropriate students find their leaves. Continue in the same way, using different instructions, until each child has found his personal leaf. As a simple and artistic follow-up, have each student press a nylon pot scrubber (or bath pouf) into fall-related colors of paint and then repeatedly press the scrubber onto a sheet of paper. Then have her glue her personalized leaf on the middle of the painting.

Roxanne LaBell Dearman
NC Early Intervention Program for Children Who Are Deaf or
    Hard of Hearing
Charlotte, NC

Group Time

Leaf Piles
Sorting

Take youngsters outside. Encourage them to gather a few fall leaves and place them in a bag. Then go inside and empty the leaves in your group-time area. Have students sit around the leaves. Say, "I notice that the leaves are different sizes." Then have students help you sort the leaves into piles by size. Once the leaves are sorted, say, "I also notice that the leaves are different colors." Place the leaves in one large pile and then have students re-sort them. Finally, ask students if there are any other ways the leaves can be sorted.

Mary Robles
Portland, OR

L Is for Leaf
Beginning sound /l/

Collect several real or fake fall leaves and place them in a gift bag. Attach tape lines to the floor to make a capital *L*. To begin, name a word. Have a child identify whether the word begins with /l/. If it does, have him remove a leaf from the bag and place it on the *L*. Continue in the same way until the entire letter is covered with leaves.

Suggested words: ladder, ladybug, lamp, kite, lemon, peanut, rain, letter, light, let, barn, lion, pear, lip, log, saw, leg, can, lavender, lift, lettuce, lace, loan, door, long, love, lamb, less, loaf, loud, fan, lap, lose

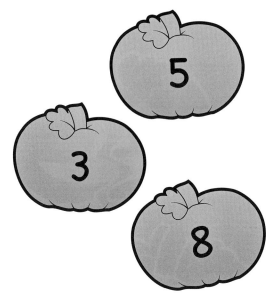

Pumpkin Patch Paces
Matching numbers

To prepare for this small-group activity, label pumpkin cutouts (pattern on page 17, enlarged) with different numbers. Attach the pumpkins to the floor so that there isn't much space between them. Get a set of number cards that match the numbers on the pumpkins. Have a child choose a number card. Then encourage him to walk carefully through the pumpkin patch, without stepping on any pumpkins, until he reaches his number. Then have him carefully return the number to you. Continue with each child in the group.

Tricia Kylene Brown
Bowling Green, KY

Write on It!
Forming the letter P, beginning sounds

Set a large pumpkin in the middle of your group-time area. Place a permanent marker nearby. Say a word (see the suggestions below). Have a child identify whether the word begins with /p/ like *pumpkin*. If it does, have her take the marker and write a letter P on the pumpkin. Continue in the same way with several other words until each child gets the opportunity to write the letter.

Suggested words: pan, pants, parachute, egg, peanut, rug, pear, pen, sail, pencil, penguin, penny, worm, piano, pie, pig, pillow, wink, pin, pipe, jeep, pizza, rabbit, pocket, popcorn, pot, pump, nut, pull, peace

Group Time

Pumpkin Match

Spatial skills, matching

Oh no! Someone must have dropped these jack-o'-lanterns! No doubt your youngsters can put them together again. Make several enlarged copies of the pumpkin pattern on page 17 and program each one with a unique face. Puzzle-cut the resulting jack-o'-lanterns. Then give each child a jack-o'-lantern half. Explain that the jack-o'-lanterns are broken and need to be put together. Then have each child find his matching jack-o'-lantern half.

Tricia Kylene Brown
Bowling Green, KY

From Seed to Pumpkin

Life cycle of a pumpkin

Get youngsters involved in the life cycle of a pumpkin with this fun pantomime. In advance, cut out a copy of the life cycle cards on page 18 and display them in your classroom in the appropriate order. Point to each card (use a pointer with a pumpkin cutout for extra fun) and describe what is happening. Next, choose a child to pantomime each step in the life cycle (see below) or have all children pantomime each step. What a fun and simple way to remember the life cycle!

Life Cycle Pantomime
seed: curl up into a little ball
sprout: sit and move arms slowly upward
vine: wiggle arms like vines
blossom: cup hands so they resemble a flower
small pumpkin: hold arms in front of you to create a small circle
big pumpkin: hold arms in front of you to create a big circle; puff out cheeks

Black, Orange, Black, Orange

Making sound patterns and object patterns

Focus on colors and symbols of the season with this patterning activity. Recite the rhyme shown. Then make an *AB* sound pattern with youngsters, with you saying "black" and students saying "orange." If desired, follow up the sound pattern by having youngsters help you arrange orange and black pom-poms to make the pattern. Repeat the rhyme, replacing the underlined words with "cats" and "bats." If desired, encourage students to help you arrange pictures of cats and bats to make the pattern.

Let's say a pattern back and forth
Just between me and you.
I'll say [orange], and you say [black].
Patterns are fun to do!

Suzanne Moore
Tucson, AZ

Upside Down?

Print awareness

Review with youngsters that bats sleep upside down. Then give each child a bat cutout (patterns on page 19) and gather student name cards. Have youngsters practice holding their bats upside down and right-side up. Then choose a name card and hold it upside down. Encourage youngsters to hold their bats upside down as well. Repeat the process with each name card, holding some names upside down and others right-side up and prompting children to hold their bats accordingly.

Roxanne LaBell Dearman
NC Early Intervention Program for Children Who Are
   Deaf or Hard of Hearing
Charlotte, NC

Group Time

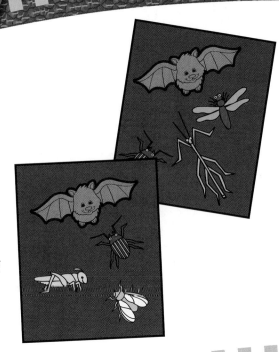

A Buggy Lunch!
Comparing sets

Youngsters compare sets of bat snacks for this small-group activity! Place two pieces of bulletin board paper on the floor. Place a bat cutout (patterns on page 19) on the corner of each sheet of paper. Get plastic bugs (or manipulatives to represent bugs) and a die. Gather a small group of youngsters around the paper (sky). To begin, have a child roll the die and count the dots. Then encourage her to place the corresponding number of bugs in the sky near one of the bats. Repeat the process with a different child and the second bat. Then have students compare the sets of bats using the words *greater*, *fewer*, and *equal*. Finally, have them count to find the number of bats altogether.

Eight Little Legs
Participating in a group game

Make a simple spider body cutout and place it on the floor. Put several jumbo wiggle eyes and eight paper strips (legs) in a basket. Gather youngsters in a circle around the body. Then lead students in singing the song as they pass the basket. When the song is finished, have the child with the basket remove a leg or an eye and place it on the spider body. Continue in the same way until the spider has all its eyes and legs.

(sung to the tune of "Clementine")

Build a spider, build a spider.
Give it legs, and give it eyes.
Build a spider, build a spider
With our spidery supplies!

Tricia Kylene Brown
Bowling Green, KY

Weather.

Weaving a Web
Beginning sound /w/

Have youngsters sit in a circle and then explain that spiders weave webs. Encourage youngsters to notice that the words *weave* and *web* begin with /w/. Next, give a child a ball of yarn. Say a word. If the word begins with /w/, have him hold the loose end of yarn and roll the ball to a classmate. If the word does not begin with /w/, the child does nothing and waits for the next word. Continue in the same way, having youngsters hold the yarn as they roll the ball until they have created their very own web!

Flying Owls
Sorting by different attributes

Gather brown and gray pom-poms (mice) in two different sizes. Then scatter a class supply of the mice around the room. Tell youngsters that they are going to pretend to be owls looking for their lunch on a chilly fall night. Then have your little owls fly around the room looking for mice. When a child finds a mouse, he picks it up and flies back to the group-time area. Then he places the mouse in a designated location and takes a seat. When each little owl is back, have them help you sort the mice by color. Next, ask if there is a different way to sort the mice, leading youngsters to conclude that the mice can be re-sorted by size. Then help students re-sort the mice.

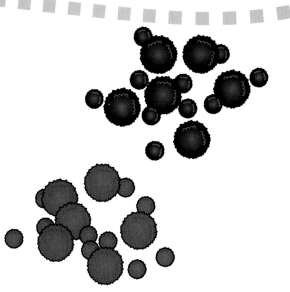

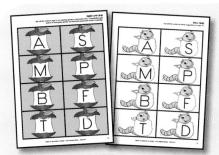

Check out the activity cards on pages 73 and 75 for practice matching letters!

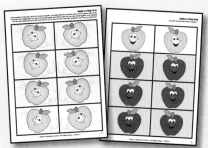

Spotlight sorting skills with the adorable cards on pages 77 and 79!

Practice patterning with the cards and strips on pages 85 and 87.

Sequencing Cards
Use with "Crunch!" on page 5.

TEC61417

TEC61417

TEC61417

TEC61417

TEC61417

Ready for September & October • ©The Mailbox® Books • TEC61417

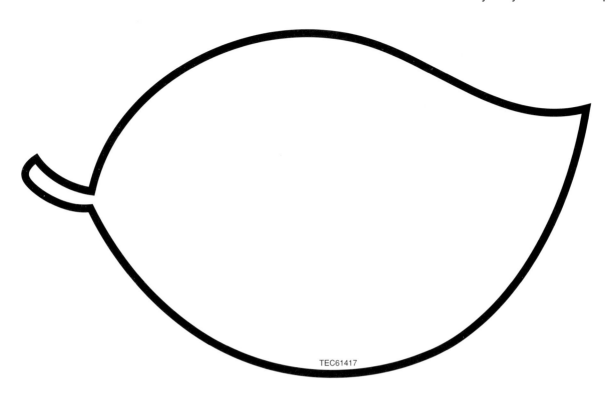

TEC61417

Pumpkin Pattern
Use with "Pumpkin Patch Paces" on page 11 and "Pumpkin Match" on page 12.

TEC61417

Pumpkin Life Cycle Cards

Use with "From Seed to Pumpkin" on page 12.

Ready for September & October • ©The Mailbox® Books • TEC61417

TEC61417

TEC61417

Songs & Such

A Friendly Welcome

This adorable action rhyme is just right for the beginning of the school year.

Welcome to school. It's a brand-new year.
It's nice to see smiling faces here.
We'll play together and learn new things.
We'll jump and run and swing on swings!

Stretch arms outward.
Move pointer fingers outward to pantomime a smile.
Clap to the beat.
Jump, run in place, and sway back and forth.

Deborah Garmon, Groton, CT

A Brand-New Year!

This easy-to-sing ditty is sure to be a favorite!

(sung to the tune of "Head and Shoulders")

Welcome to a brand-new year, brand-new year!
There is nothing you should fear, you should fear.
Let's all give a happy preschool cheer!
I'm so glad that you are here, you are here!

Apples for Lunch

Use repositionable adhesive to attach five apple cutouts to a wall. Then lead students in performing this adorable action chant five times, reducing the number of apples by one each time. Finally, perform the final verse.

[Five] red apples hanging on the tree,
Boy oh boy, they look good to me.
I picked one off—then crunch, crunch, crunch.
I ate that apple for my lunch.

Hold up [*five*] fingers.
Rub hands together.
Move hands open and shut like a mouth.
Rub tummy.

Final verse:
No red apples hanging on the tree.
I ate them all for lunch, you see.
But those green apples soon will be
Big, red apples just for me!

Shake head.
Rub tummy.
Point up.
Point thumb at yourself.

Chelsea Reid, M&M's Play Based Learning, Calgary, Alberta, Canada

Pick and Eat

Youngsters are sure to enjoy this song about a favorite fall activity—picking apples! During the second verse, scatter red pom-poms (apples) around the students. Then, during the third verse, invite them to pick up the apples and place them in a container.

(sung to the tune of "The Mulberry Bush")

Here we go round the apple tree,
The apple tree, the apple tree.
Here we go round the apple tree
On an autumn morning.

This is the way we shake the tree,
Shake the tree, shake the tree.
This is the way we shake the tree
On an autumn morning.

This is the way we pick the apples,
Pick the apples, pick the apples.
This is the way we pick the apples
On an autumn morning.

This is the way we eat the apples,
Eat the apples, eat the apples.
This is the way we eat the apples
On an autumn morning.

Chelsea Reid

Songs & Such

Wonderful Me

Use this rhyme to encourage youngsters to celebrate their special qualities. After saying the rhyme with students, invite each child to name a personal quality that makes her wonderful.

I have two eyes, *Point to eyes.*
A little nose too, *Touch nose.*
A mouth that makes *Touch mouth.*
Smiles for you.   *Move pointer fingers outward to*
        pantomime a smile

I have ten fingers *Wiggle fingers.*
And ten toes, you see. *Point to toes.*
So here I am now. *Stretch arms outward.*
It's wonderful me! *Point to self.*

Deborah Garmon
Groton, CT

I Am Special

Prior to singing the song with students, divide students into groups based on their eye color. Then lead each group in singing the song, being sure to insert the correct eye color.

(sung to the tune of "Twinkle, Twinkle, Little Star)

I am special, you will see.
There is no one else like me.
I have [brown] eyes and a nose,
Ten strong fingers and ten toes.
I am special, you will see.
Let's be good friends, you and me.

Deborah Garmon

A Big Thank-You

Celebrate the many wonderful things that grandparents do every day with this adorable song. After singing the song, invite each child to name something that a grandparent or special older friend does for him.

(sung to the tune of "The Farmer in the Dell")

Grandparents [hold our hands].
Grandparents [hold our hands].
Thank you for all you do!
Grandparents [hold our hands].

Continue with the following: *have big hearts, make us smile, tell us stories*

Roxanne LaBell Dearman
NC Early Intervention Program for Children Who Are Deaf or Hard
    of Hearing, Charlotte, NC

To Grandparents With Love

Here's a rhyme that is sure to make youngsters' grandparents feel special on National Grandparents Day.

We love our grandparents every day.   *Hug self.*
They make us happy in every way.   *Use pointer fingers to pantomime a smile.*
Grandparents are special every day of the year.   *Count on fingers.*
But on Grandparents Day, they're especially dear!   *Hug self.*

Deborah Garmon
Groton, CT

Songs & Such

Signs of Fall

Prior to singing this toe-tapping ditty with little ones, invite each child to draw a picture that shows his favorite thing about fall. Encourage volunteers to share their drawings with their classmates. Then lead youngsters in singing the song.

(sung to the tune of "The Farmer in the Dell")

[The leaves are falling down],
[The leaves are falling down].
Summer's fun, but fall's begun.
[The leaves are falling down].

Continue with the following:
The weather has a chill.
The squirrels will bury food.
The pumpkins are so big.
I really love the fall.

Cynthia Holcomb, San Angelo, TX

Little Squirrels

Youngsters are sure to enjoy singing this song about these adorable critters. For added fun, have each child make a simple squirrel stick puppet. Then encourage students to move their puppets about as you lead them in singing the song.

(sung to the tune of
"If You're Happy and You Know It")

Oh, the little squirrels are running all around,
Digging holes and putting acorns in the ground.
They are quick as quick can be
As they scamper round a tree.
Oh, the little squirrels are running all around.

Deborah Garmon
Groton, CT

Dancing Leaves

Here's a delightful action song that's just perfect for fall! When youngsters are comfortable singing the song, encourage them to sing as they pretend to be dancing leaves.

(sung to the tune of "Are You Sleeping?")

Leaves are falling,
Leaves are falling,
From the trees,
From the trees.
They dance all around,
Falling to the ground.
Dancing leaves
In the breeze.

Deborah Garmon, Groton, CT

Time to Rake

Encourage youngsters to pretend they are raking leaves as you lead them in singing this entertaining song.

(sung to the tune of "Old MacDonald Had a Farm")

Autumn leaves fall off the trees.
It's that time of year.
When all the leaves come down, we know
Raking time is near.
With a rake, rake here and a rake, rake there.
Here a rake, there a rake,
Everybody rake, rake!
Autumn leaves fall off the trees.
It's that time of year.

Deborah Garmon

Songs & Such

Fire Facts

Youngsters review some important fire safety rules with this catchy little song.

(sung to the tune of "Sing a Song of Sixpence")

Never play with matches.
It's not the thing to do.
Matches can start fires.
They are not safe for you.
If you see a fire,
Quickly walk or run.
Find someone and ask them,
"Will you please call 9-1-1?"

Deborah Garmon
Groton, CT

Pretty Pumpkins

This adorable song is just right to use during a unit about pumpkins.

(sung to the tune of "The Itsy-Bitsy Spider")

I saw a little pumpkin growing on the ground.   *Point.*
It grew on some vines that wiggled all around.   *Wiggle fingers.*
The pumpkin was so small and green as green can be.   *Clasp hands.*
Then it changed from green to orange—a lovely thing to see!   *Hold arms out as if holding a large pumpkin.*

Deborah Garmon

Growing Pumpkins

Little ones learn how pumpkins grow with this catchy song. If desired, invite students to add actions.

(sung to the tune of "Clementine")

Pumpkin shopping, pumpkin shopping,
I am looking for the best!
You should stand out from the others
And be better than the rest.

Are you big, and are you orange
With a stem so tall and green?
You'll be perfect in the window
Shining when it's Halloween.

A Batty Nap

Here's a fun song about those bug-eating nocturnal critters—bats!

(sung to the tune of "Head and Shoulders")

Bats sleep upside down all day, all the day.
Then at night they fly away, fly away.
They eat bugs all night along the way.
Then they sleep all of the day—upside down!

Suzanne Moore
Tucson, AZ

Songs & Such

Spider's Lunch!

Spotlight the perfect spider meal with this entertaining sing-along!

(sung to the tune of "Did You Ever See a Lassie?")

Did you ever see a spider,
A spider, a spider?
Did you ever see a spider
Catch bugs for its lunch?
It finds them so yummy!
Just right for its tummy!
Did you ever see a spider
Catch bugs for its lunch?

Halloween Sights

Here's a song that's just perfect for the Halloween season. Color and cut apart a copy of the cards on page 29 and place them in a plastic pumpkin. Ask a volunteer to take a card and show it to the group. After discussing what is on the card, lead youngsters in singing the song, inserting the words on the card where indicated. Continue with the remaining cards.

(sung to the tune of "The Muffin Man")

What will we see on Halloween,
On Halloween, on Halloween?
What will we see on Halloween?
We'll see [one yellow moon]!

Cynthia Holcomb
San Angelo, TX

1 yellow moon

TEC61417

2 hairy feet

TEC61417

3 cuddly cats

TEC61417

4 little owls

TEC61417

5 happy smiles

TEC61417

6 flying bats

TEC61417

Centers

Dramatic-Play Area

Welcome to Preschool!

Stage your dramatic-play area so it resembles a mini classroom. Provide a desk (teacher's desk); student chairs; and items like a wipe-off board and markers, a small pointer, puzzles, storybooks, puppets, and dolls. Youngsters use the props to engage in teacher-student classroom play. *Community helper role-playing*

Tricia Kylene Brown
Bowling Green, KY

Math Center

Back-to-School Backpack

Trace school-related items, such as a box of crayons, a storybook, a squeeze bottle of glue, a ruler, and children's safety scissors on a sheet of poster board. Then put the items in a backpack and place the backpack and poster board at the center. A child takes an item from the backpack and places it atop the matching outline. He repeats the process with each remaining item. *Visual discrimination*

GLUE

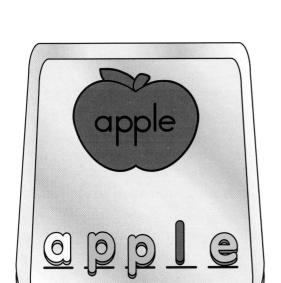

A-P-P-L-E

Label an apple cutout (patterns on page 45) as shown and attach it to a cookie sheet. Use a permanent marker to draw five lines below the apple. (Hint: When you wish to remove the marker from the sheet, simply use rubbing alcohol.) Place the tray at a center along with magnetic letters to spell *apple*. A child points to the letter *a* in *apple*; then she finds the corresponding magnetic letter and attaches it to the sheet. She repeats the process with each remaining letter. **Matching letters**

Roxanne LaBell Dearman
NC Early Intervention Program for Children Who Are Deaf or Hard
    of Hearing
Charlotte, NC

Wiggle Worm

Randomly punch holes in several tagboard apple cutouts (patterns on page 45). Place the apples at a center along with a length of thick green yarn (worm) for each apple. A youngster wiggles a worm onto an apple and then weaves the worm in and out of the holes. As he works, he chants, "Wiggle, wiggle, munch, munch, crunch an apple for your lunch!" **Fine-motor skills**

Roxanne LaBell Dearman

Centers

Sets of Seeds

Label cutout copies of the apple patterns on page 45 with desired numbers and matching dot sets. Place the apples at a center along with a supply of black mini pom-poms (seeds). A child takes an apple, counts out the corresponding number of seeds, and places them on the cutout, covering each dot in the set. She repeats the process with each remaining apple. When she's finished, she removes the seeds from each apple, counting them as she works. **Number recognition, counting, making sets**

Roxanne LaBell Dearman
NC Early Intervention Program for Children Who Are Deaf or Hard
   of Hearing
Charlotte, NC

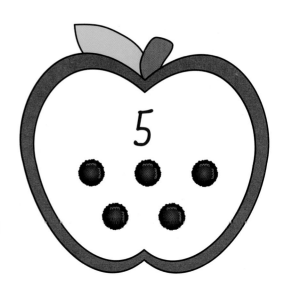

Sensory Center

Apples to Apples

Cut in half apples in different sizes and shapes. (Remove any loose seeds.) Sprinkle the cut halves with lemon juice. Provide paper plates. A child chooses an apple half and explores its color, size, shape, texture, and smell. Then he examines the remaining apples to find the matching half. To confirm that two halves are from the same apple, he holds them together to see if the sizes and shapes match. Then he places the matching halves on a plate and repeats the process. **Exploring the senses**

Roxanne LaBell Dearman

Block Center

My Family and Me

Trim around a full-length photo of each child. Attach the photos to individual cardboard tubes or wood blocks. Place the resulting figures in your block area along with toy family figures and appropriately sized toy vehicles and pets. A student visits the center and uses blocks to build a house. Then he uses the props to engage in pretend family-related play. ***Exploring family roles***

Tricia Kylene Brown
Bowling Green, KY

Writing Center

Navigating My Name

For each child, program a large sheet of construction paper with her name. Provide small toy vehicles, large craft feathers, chopsticks, pipe cleaners, and other manipulatives. Place the manipulatives near shallow containers of paint. A child dips a manipulative in the paint and then drags it over each letter in her name. She repeats the process with different manipulatives. ***Forming letters***

Tricia Kylene Brown

Centers

That's My Number!

Give each child a personalized cell phone cutout (patterns on page 46) along with an index card labeled with his name and phone number. Provide a yellow ink pad. Using his card as a reference, he "dials" his number by pressing his fingertip on the ink pad and then onto the appropriate numbers on the key pad. *Matching numbers*

Tricia Kylene Brown
Bowling Green, KY

I am one of a kind!

One of a Kind

Program a class supply of white construction paper with the words shown. Provide a marker or crayon, an ink pad, and a magnifying glass. A child traces one hand onto a programmed paper. She presses her fingertip on the ink pad and then on the corresponding fingertip tracing. She continues with each remaining finger on that hand and then repeats the process with her other hand. When she's finished, she uses the magnifying glass to examine her fingerprints. *Fine-motor skills, making observations*

Climb the Ladder

For this partner activity, give each child a fire truck cutout (patterns on page 47), a toy person (firefighter), and 12 connecting cubes. Scatter number cards from 5 to 12 face-down. A child flips a card and identifies the number; then each child connects that many cubes to make a ladder. Next, each youngster places the ladder on his truck and helps the firefighter "climb" to the top, counting each cube as he climbs. Then students disassemble the ladders and repeat the process, taking turns to flip the remaining cards. ***Identifying numbers, counting, making sets***

Pamela B. Szeliga, Relay Elementary, Baltimore, MD

Block Center

To the Rescue!

Attach flame cutouts to blocks and place them at your block center along with pieces of garden hose (fire hose), toy fire engines, and plastic toy people. A child creates buildings out of blocks, using the flame-decorated blocks as desired. Then he uses the props for pretend firefighter play. ***Spatial skills, community helper role-playing***

Centers

Literacy Center

Make a Match

For this small-group game, label pairs of flame cutouts with matching letters. Scatter the flames facedown. To play, a student turns over two flames. If the letters match, youngsters pretend to spray the flames with water; then the student who flipped the flames sets them aside. If the letters do not match, he turns the flames back over. Play continues, in turn, until there are no flames left. ***Matching letters***

adapted from an idea by Tricia Kylene Brown
Bowling Green, KY

Water Table

Call 9-1-1!

In your water table, float craft foam flames labeled as shown. Display near the table a sign that says "9-1-1." Provide a spray bottle filled with water. A child pretends the flames are real and calls out, "I see flames; call 9-1-1!" squirting the matching flame with water as she says each number. She repeats the activity until interest wanes. ***Safety awareness, number recognition***

Tricia Kylene Brown

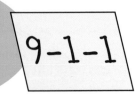

Leaf Blower

Mark a masking tape line on one end of a table and personalize a plastic drinking straw for each child. Provide a real or silk leaf. A student places the leaf behind the line and then blows through her straw to move the leaf. She manipulates her breath and body position, helping her to blow the leaf along the length of the table and off the opposite end. She repeats the activity without the straw and then decides which method is more effective in controlling the leaf. *Cause and effect, oral-motor skills*

Roxanne LaBell Dearman
NC Early Intervention Program for Children Who Are Deaf or Hard of Hearing
Charlotte, NC

Math Center

Leaves Are Falling

Place a large tree cutout on the floor. Provide a bag containing ten craft foam leaves. A student holds the bag a few feet above the tree and then spills the leaves from the bag. She visually scans the area and guesses whether more leaves landed on the tree or on the floor. Then she counts the leaves ⟍⟍ her guess. *Counting, comparing*

Roxanne LaBell Dearman

38

Centers

Hidden Beneath the Leaves

Fill your sensory table or a large plastic tub with real or silk leaves; then hide several items under the leaves. Place a tray nearby with a number card that shows how many objects are hidden. A youngster searches through the leaves and finds an item. She removes the object from the table, identifies the item, and then places it on the tray. She continues until all the objects are found, counting the collection each time she adds an item to the tray. *Number recognition, counting*

adapted from an idea by Darlene Butler Taig
Willow Creek Preschool
Westland, MI

5

Play Dough Center

Leaves and Acorns

Place at a table a laminated tree cutout minus foliage, a leaf-shaped cookie cutter, brown pom-poms (acorns), and play dough in fall-related colors. A child uses the cookie cutter and play dough to add foliage to the tree and area around the tree (ground). When he's finished, he puts acorns on the tree and scatters some on the ground! *Fine-motor skills*

adapted from an idea by Roxanne LaBell Dearman
NC Early Intervention for Children Who Are Deaf or
    Hard of Hearing
Charlotte, NC

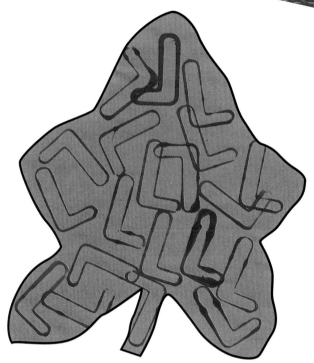

L Is for Leaf

Set out red, yellow, and orange construction paper leaf cutouts. Also provide a plastic letter *L* and a paper plate with a thin layer of brown paint. A student dips the letter in the paint and then presses it onto the leaf, chanting "*L* is for *leaf*, /l/, /l/, /l/!" as he works. He continues until his leaf is covered with *L*s. **Letter-sound association**

Roxanne LaBell Dearman
NC Early Intervention for Children Who Are Deaf or
   Hard of Hearing
Charlotte, NC

How Many Acorns?

For each child, divide a sheet of paper into four sections. Provide a die and a brown ink pad. Station an adult at the center. A child takes a paper. If desired, provide a squirrel puppet, figurine, or stuffed toy. The adult asks the child to find out how many acorns Sammy Squirrel buried on Monday. The child rolls the die and counts the dots. She makes that many fingerprints in one of the sections on the paper. The adult presents scenarios for different days, and the youngster continues until each section has a set of acorns. Then the adult helps her draw acorn caps and stems on the fingerprints. If desired, the adult can ask her questions about the sets, such as "Which set has the most acorns?" **Comparing sets**

Centers

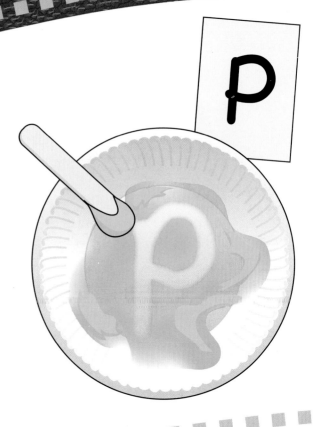

P Is for Pumpkin

Place at a table a bowl of canned pumpkin, a spoon, disposable plastic plates, and craft sticks. Also display a letter *P*. A student puts a dollop or two of pumpkin on a plate, spreads the pumpkin with a craft stick, and then uses the stick to write *P* in the pumpkin. He smooths out the pumpkin with the craft stick and then repeats the process. **As an alternative**, put canned pumpkin in a resealable plastic bag and reinforce the seal with packing tape. A youngster writes the letter *P* in the sealed pumpkin using his fingertip. ***Letter formation***

adapted from an idea by Tricia Kylene Brown
Bowling Green, KY

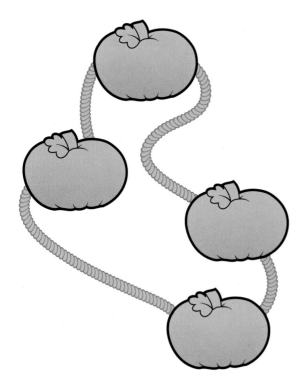

Gross-Motor Area

Pumpkin Patch Promenade

Attach several large pumpkin cutouts to the floor; then connect the pumpkins with green yarn or crepe paper streamers (vines) to create a mock pumpkin patch. A youngster uses a variety of gross-motor movements—such as walking, hopping, tiptoeing, sidestepping, and marching—to maneuver through the pumpkin patch, trying to step over the vines and pumpkins as she goes. ***Gross-motor skills***

Tricia Kylene Brown

Science Center

Hairy the Jack-o'-Lantern

Place at your science center orange disposable cups, black paper scraps, and glue. Also provide potting soil, grass seed, a scoop, and water. A child tears facial features from the paper scraps and glues them on the cup. Next, he uses the scoop to fill the cup with soil. Then he sprinkles grass seed on the soil and adds water. He places the project near a window and checks the soil daily to see if it needs water. Then he observes his project as it grows green "hair"! ***Caring for a living thing, observation skills***

Mary Robles
Ardenwald Elementary
Milwaukie, OR

Fine-Motor Area

Pound the Pumpkin

Place at a table a large pumpkin, a supply of golf tees, a small rubber mallet, and a pair of pliers. A youngster uses the mallet to pound golf tees into the pumpkin. When she's finished, she uses the pliers to remove the tees. ***Hand-eye coordination, fine-motor and gross-motor skills***

Darlene Butler Taig
Willow Creek Preschool
Westland, MI

Centers

Sensory Center

Sensational Pumpkin Stuff!

Stock your sensory area with pumpkin-related items that appeal to all the senses. For example, provide pumpkin bread and pumpkin cookies for youngsters to taste, sprinkle cotton balls with pumpkin spice for students to smell, and set out pumpkin innards for children to feel and examine. For added fun, provide a solid pumpkin and a gutted pumpkin for children to knock on and decide if the sounds they hear are the same! ***Exploring the senses***

Tricia Kylene Brown, Bowling Green, KY
Mary Robles, Ardenwald Elementary, Milwaukie, OR

Play Dough Center

Spicy Pumpkin Treats

Set out orange play dough scented with pumpkin spice, black play dough (for making jack-o'-lantern features), pumpkin-shaped cookie cutters, a cookie sheet, and a rolling pin. If desired, provide a holiday-related apron and oven mitts. A youngster uses the play dough and props to pretend to make pumpkin and jack-o'-lantern cookies. ***Fine-motor skills***

Tricia Kylene Brown

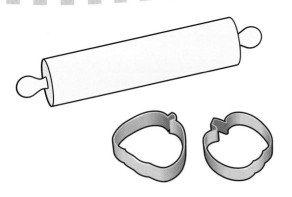

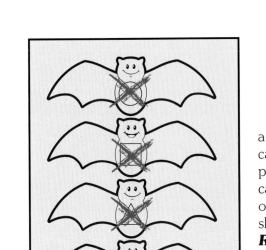

To the Bat Cave!

Tape a cutout copy of the bats on page 48 to the underside of a table; then drape a dark bed sheet or blanket over the table (bat cave). Give each child who visits the cave a crayon and a copy of page 48. Also provide a flashlight. A youngster crawls into the cave and shines the flashlight onto a bat. She studies the shape on the bat's body, and then crosses out the bat with the matching shape on her paper. She continues until each bat is crossed out. *Recognizing shapes*

Roxanne LaBell Dearman
NC Early Intervention for Children Who Are Deaf or Hard of Hearing
Charlotte, NC

Writing Center

Night Flight

Twist the center of a black pipe cleaner around a pencil; then shape the loose ends so they resemble bat wings. Place the bat pencil at your writing center along with a black paper strip programmed as shown. A student uses the pencil to trace along the line, pretending that the bat is flying to the cave. *Developing one's pencil grip, eye-hand coordination*

Roxanne LaBell Dearman

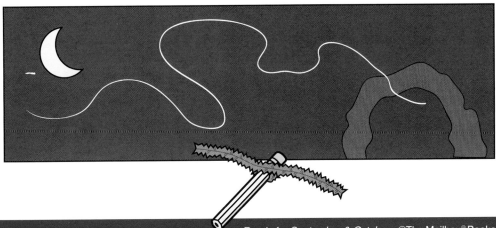

Centers

Math Center

Web of Spiders

For this small-group game, provide a tagboard spiderweb, a supply of plastic spiders, and a large die. A player rolls the die, counts aloud the dots, and then places that many spiders on the web. Play continues, in turn, until all the spiders are on the web. (Note: A player must roll the same number of dots as spiders to finish the game.) **Counting**

adapted from an idea by Tricia Kylene Brown
Bowling Green, KY

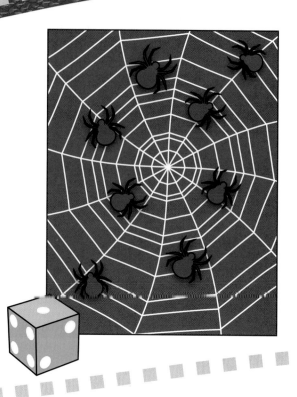

Literacy Center

The Perfect Limb

For this partner game, make several copies of page 49. Label each pattern with matching letters as shown, making the letters on each pattern different from the others. Cut the owls and limbs apart and scatter them facedown in two separate piles. A youngster turns over a limb and an owl. If the letters match, he says, "Whoo! Whoo!" as he flies the owl through the air and lands it on the limb. If the letters do not match, he turns the cutouts back over. Play continues, in turn, until each owl is on the appropriate limb. **Matching letters**

Tricia Kylene Brown

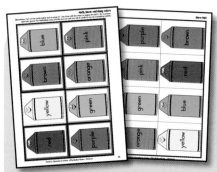

Check out the math game on pages 65–71 for practice matching colors!

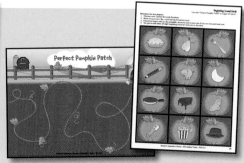

Spotlight beginning sounds with the mats and cards on pages 89–94!

Practice sequencing with the cards on page 95.

Use with "Pick One!" on page 7, "*A-P-P-L-E*" and "Wiggle Worm" on page 31 and "Sets of Seeds" on page 32.

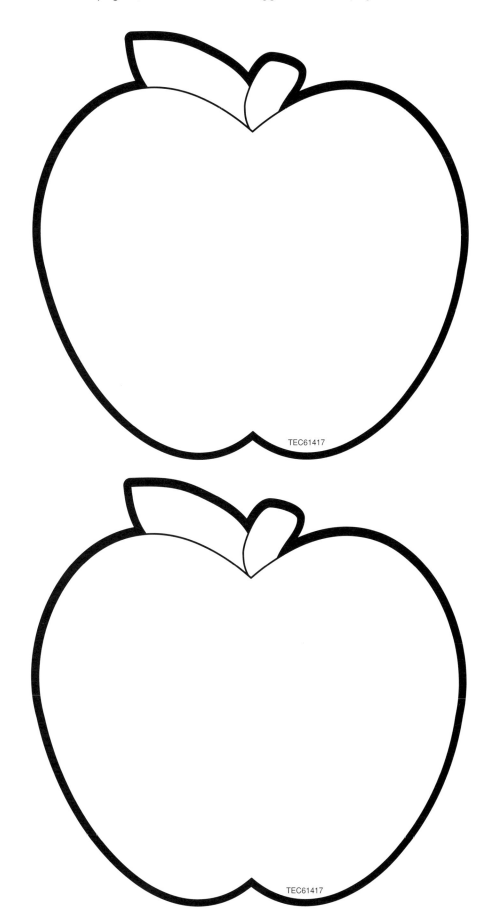

TEC61417

TEC61417

Cell Phone Patterns

Use with "That's My Number!" on page 34.

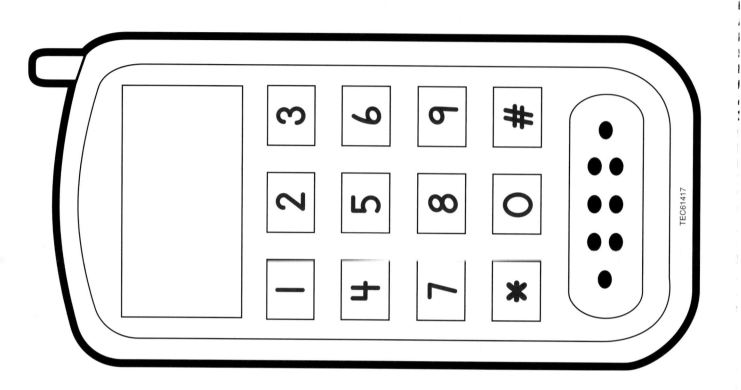

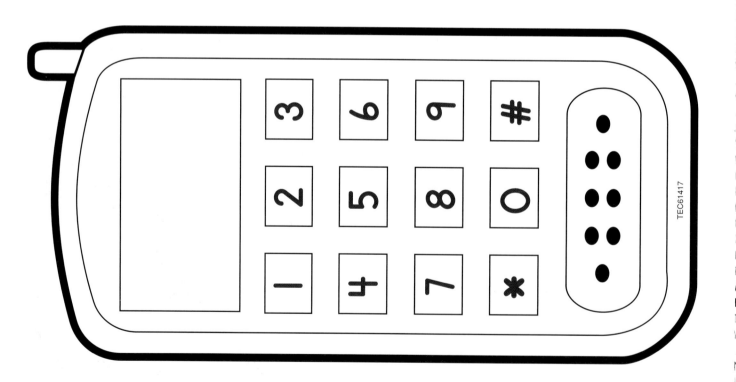

TEC61417

TEC61417

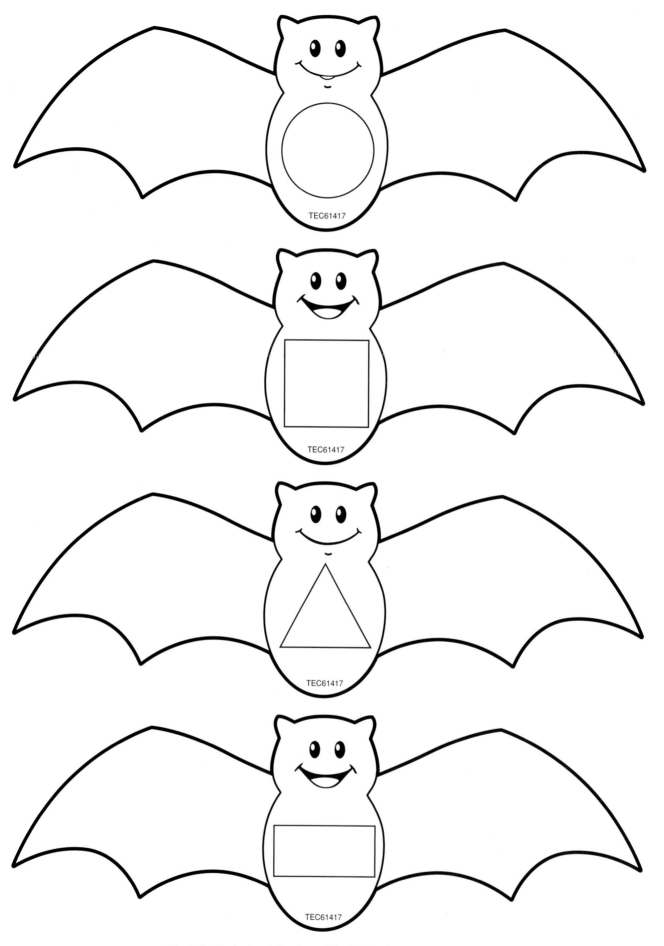

TEC61417

TEC61417

TEC61417

TEC61417

Ready for September & October • ©The Mailbox® Books • TEC61417

Note to the teacher: Use with "To the Bat Cave!" on page 43.

TEC61417

TEC61417

Arts & Crafts

Shining Stars

Little ones get a surprise when they complete this back-to-school craft. Use a white crayon to personalize a white star cutout. On the first day of school, have youngsters brush yellow watercolors over the entire star. As each child paints, prompt her to watch what magically appears on the paper. After the paint dries, display the stars on a space-themed board titled "Preschool Is Out of This World!"

Janet Boyce
Cokato, MN

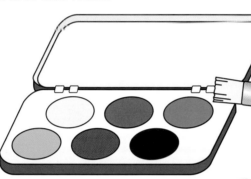

Marvelous Me!

To make this adorable self-likeness, staple a small paper plate to a large paper plate half. Color the small plate (head) to match your skin tone. Then look in a mirror and draw facial features to match. Next, glue paper shreds to the head so they resemble your hair. Then color the plate half so it resembles a favorite shirt.

Janet Boyce

My Banner

In advance, send home a copy of page 61 with each child. Ask the family to help her complete the sheet. Then have the family return it to school along with a photograph of the child. Trim the corners of a sheet of construction paper for each child. Then glue the page and photo to the paper. Have her add self-adhesive craft foam shapes and stickers to the paper.

Janet Boyce, Cokato, MN

An Attractive Gift!

These handmade magnets make perfect gifts for National Grandparents Day! To make one, trace one hand onto colorful tagboard and then cut out the tracing. Use crayons or markers to draw designs on the hand cutout. Then fold down the ring and middle fingers so the cutout makes the American Sign Language sign for I LOVE YOU. Add designs to the folded-down fingers. To complete the project, add a magnet to the back of the hand.

Janet Boyce

Arts & Crafts

Process Art

Apples Every Which Way

Cut apples in a variety of different ways to make halves, slices, and chunks. Stick a plastic fork in each apple piece. Dip an apple piece in paint and make a print on a sheet of white construction paper. Continue to make prints using different apple pieces and paint colors.

Janet Boyce, Cokato, MN

Just the Core!

In advance, trim the edge of a paper plate as shown. Then tear pieces out of the sides of the trimmed plate so it resembles an apple core. Paint the top and bottom of the core to show your favorite apple color. After the paint dries, tear five apple seeds from black paper and glue them to the plate. Then tear a stem from brown paper and glue it to the top of the apple.

Janet Boyce

51

All About Me!

My name is **Eva Jameson**.

I am **4** years old.

My birthday is **March 12**.

My favorite color is

My favorite food is **macaroni and cheese**

I have **2** pets.

My favorite activity is **playing with my friend Jacob at his house**.

My Banner

In advance, send home a copy of page 61 with each child. Ask the family to help her complete the sheet. Then have the family return it to school along with a photograph of the child. Trim the corners of a sheet of construction paper for each child. Then glue the page and photo to the paper. Have her add self-adhesive craft foam shapes and stickers to the paper.

Janet Boyce, Cokato, MN

An Attractive Gift!

These handmade magnets make perfect gifts for National Grandparents Day! To make one, trace one hand onto colorful tagboard and then cut out the tracing. Use crayons or markers to draw designs on the hand cutout. Then fold down the ring and middle fingers so the cutout makes the American Sign Language sign for I LOVE YOU. Add designs to the folded-down fingers. To complete the project, add a magnet to the back of the hand.

Janet Boyce

Arts & Crafts

Process Art

Apples Every Which Way

Cut apples in a variety of different ways to make halves, slices, and chunks. Stick a plastic fork in each apple piece. Dip an apple piece in paint and make a print on a sheet of white construction paper. Continue to make prints using different apple pieces and paint colors.

Janet Boyce, Cokato, MN

Just the Core!

In advance, trim the edge of a paper plate as shown. Then tear pieces out of the sides of the trimmed plate so it resembles an apple core. Paint the top and bottom of the core to show your favorite apple color. After the paint dries, tear five apple seeds from black paper and glue them to the plate. Then tear a stem from brown paper and glue it to the top of the apple.

Janet Boyce

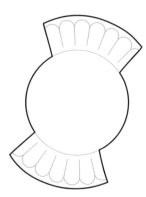

Applesauce Art

To prepare for this process art activity, pour applesauce into a sieve and let it drain overnight. Mix equal parts of drained applesauce and white glue. Divide the mixture into three containers and then stir a few drops of food coloring into each container. Scoop dollops of each paint color onto a sheet of white construction paper. Then use the back of a spoon to mix and spread the paint to make designs. Set the project aside to dry for several days.

Janet Boyce, Cokato, MN

Flash the Fire Dog

This craft is the perfect way to finish up a fire safety unit. Draw a dog face on the bottom of a small paper plate. Cut ears from white construction paper. Press a cork into a shallow pan of black paint and then make prints on the ears and face so the dog resembles a dalmatian. Attach a cutout copy of a fire helmet from page 62 to the project. To complete the project, tape a large craft stick to the back to make a puppet. Use the Flash the Fire Dog puppet to tell others about fire safety.

Arts & Crafts

Process Art

Fabulous Fall Foliage

Prepare two containers of tinted water: one yellow and one red. On a sheet of white construction paper, draw a tree with bare branches. Then drip drops of water from each container around the branches and the bottom of the tree. After a desired effect is reached, set the paper aside to dry.

Janet Boyce, Cokato, MN

Process Art

Paint and Print

Gather several artificial leaves with raised veins and stems and fall-related colors of paint. Use a wide foam paintbrush to paint the raised side of a leaf and then press the leaf on a sheet of paper to make a print. Continue making prints until a desired effect is achieved.

Janet Boyce

A Colorful Collage

To make this eye-catching craft, tear pieces of fall-colored tissue paper so they resemble fall leaves. Then brush diluted glue on a length of waxed paper and place the leaves on the glue, pressing them down on the waxed paper. To complete the collage, brush another layer of diluted glue over the leaves.

Janet Boyce, Cokato, MN

Lovely Leaves

Remove the bottom from a paper lunch bag and set it aside to use with another craft. Then cut along a crease of the bag and lay the resulting piece of paper flat. Squeeze lines of red paint on one half of the paper and lines of yellow paint on the other half. Then fold the paper in half, pat it, and unfold it. When the paint is dry, refold the paper and draw the outline of a large leaf. Cutting through both thicknesses of paper, cut out the leaf shape. Tape a yarn loop to the unpainted side of one leaf. Finally, glue the leaves together, painted-sides out.

Janet Boyce

Falling Leaves

Color a copy of page 63. Tear fall-colored tissue paper into small pieces. Then crumple the pieces (leaves) and place them on the tree without gluing them down. Squeeze a thin line of glue along the edges of your paper. Then gently place a piece of clear cellophane sized to the paper on top of the project. After the glue dries, manipulate the project so the leaves are on the tree; then move it and watch the leaves fall. For added fun, shake the project from side to side so it looks like a windy day.

Mary Robles
Ardenwald Elementary
Milwaukie, OR

Pumpkin Print Wreath

For this simple fall craft, cut a small pumpkin in half and remove the seeds and pulp. Dip a pumpkin half in a shallow container of orange paint and make prints on a large paper circle with the center cut out. After the paint dries, add a raffia bow and a yarn loop for hanging.

Mary Robles

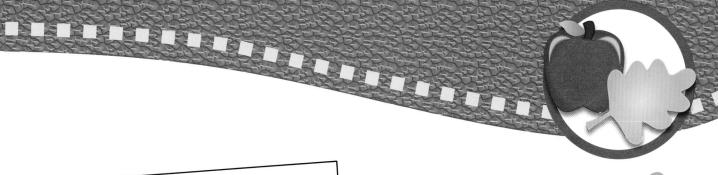

The Perfect Pumpkin

Pumpkin Seed Painting

In advance, hot-glue a dried pumpkin seed to a length of string. (Hot glue is for teacher use only.) To make this process art, color the stem on a copy of page 64. Next, dip the seed into a container of orange paint and then drag it across the pumpkin. Continue until a desired effect is reached.

Janet Boyce
Cokato, MN

A Shapely Patch

To make these adorable pumpkins, dip shaped cookie cutters into a shallow container of orange paint and make prints on a sheet of paper. After the paint dries, add stems, leaves, and vines to the prints so they resemble pumpkins in a patch. To complete the project, draw a funny jack-o'-lantern face on each pumpkin.

Janet Boyce

Arts & Crafts

Jolly Jack-o'-Lanterns

Paint the inside of a clear plastic cup orange. After the paint is dry, place the cup upside down. Then glue two black construction paper eyes, a nose, and a mouth to the cup. Next, glue a construction paper stem and leaf to the jack-o'-lantern. Finally, place a battery-operated tea light under the jack-o'-lantern and watch it glow!

Mary Robles
Ardenwald, Elementary
Milwaukie, OR

Sound Asleep

To make the owl bodies, trim a large and small paper plate as shown. Use a thick brown crayon without a wrapper to rub both sides of each plate. Then draw closed eyes and a beak on each owl. Next, fringe-cut the ridged areas (wings) of each owl body. Fold the wings of each owl so they overlap in front of the owl's face. Finally, stand the owls so the little one is inside the big one's protective wings.

Janet Boyce
Cokato, MN

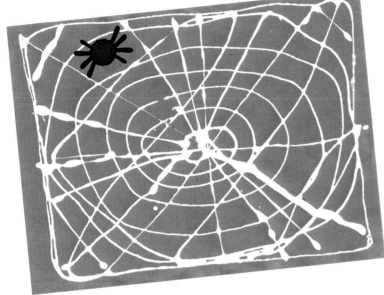

Web Designs

Mix equal parts white glue and white paint and then pour the mixture into a squeeze bottle. Squeeze lines of the glue mixture on a sheet of purple construction paper to make a web. After the glue mixture dries, glue a large black pom-pom to the web. Use a black marker to add eight legs to the pom-pom so it resembles a spider.

Janet Boyce
Cokato, MN

Crazy Legs

Lay a sheet of 9" x 12" paper horizontally. Then draw a pencil line two inches from the top. Fold the paper in half three times vertically and then unfold it to reveal eight sections. Cut along each fold line, stopping at the pencil line. Above the line, attach two hole reinforcers (eyes) and use a white crayon to draw a mouth. Then accordion-fold each strip. Next, tape the ends of the paper together. Then tape a yarn handle to the top of the spider.

Janet Boyce

Arts & Crafts

Bats in a Cave

Tear strips of brown tissue paper and glue them to a 9" x 12" sheet of construction paper so they resemble stalactites and stalagmites. To make bats, fold several 1" x 2½" paper strips as shown. Glue the bats to the paper. Then attach two yellow hole-punch dots (eyes) to each bat and use a marker to add a black dot to each eye.

Janet Boyce
Cokato, MN

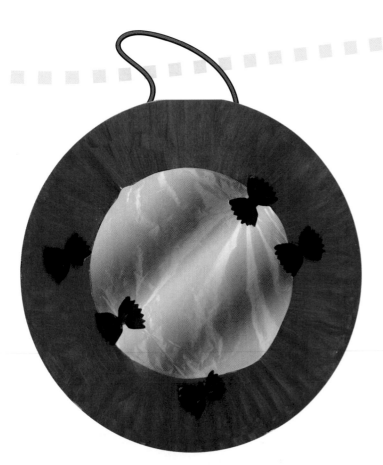

A Batty Mobile

Cut the center from a paper plate and then paint the bottom side of the remaining rim blue. Also paint several pieces of bow-tie pasta (bats) black. After the paint dries, glue the paper plate to an aluminum foil circle so it shows through the hole. Then glue the bats to the project. Finally, staple a loop of yarn to the project for hanging.

Janet Boyce

All About Me!

My name is _____.

I am _____ years old.

My birthday is _____.

My favorite color is  .

My favorite food is .

I have _____ pets.

My favorite activity is _____

_____.

Fire Helmet Patterns

Use with "Flash the Fire Dog" on page 53.

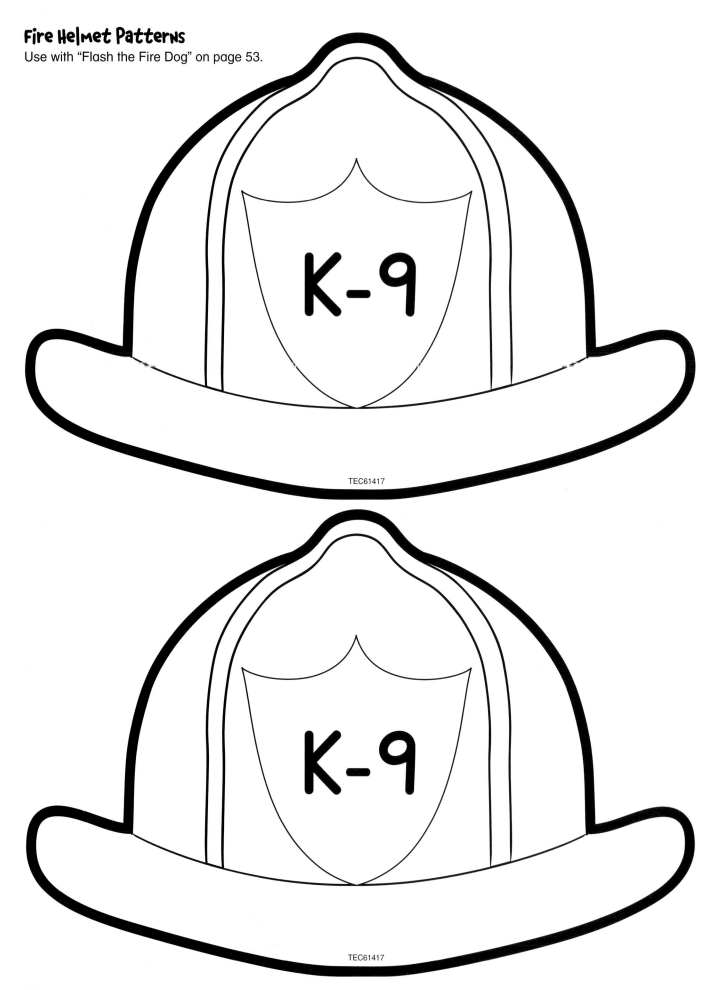

TEC61417

TEC61417

The Perfect Pumpkin

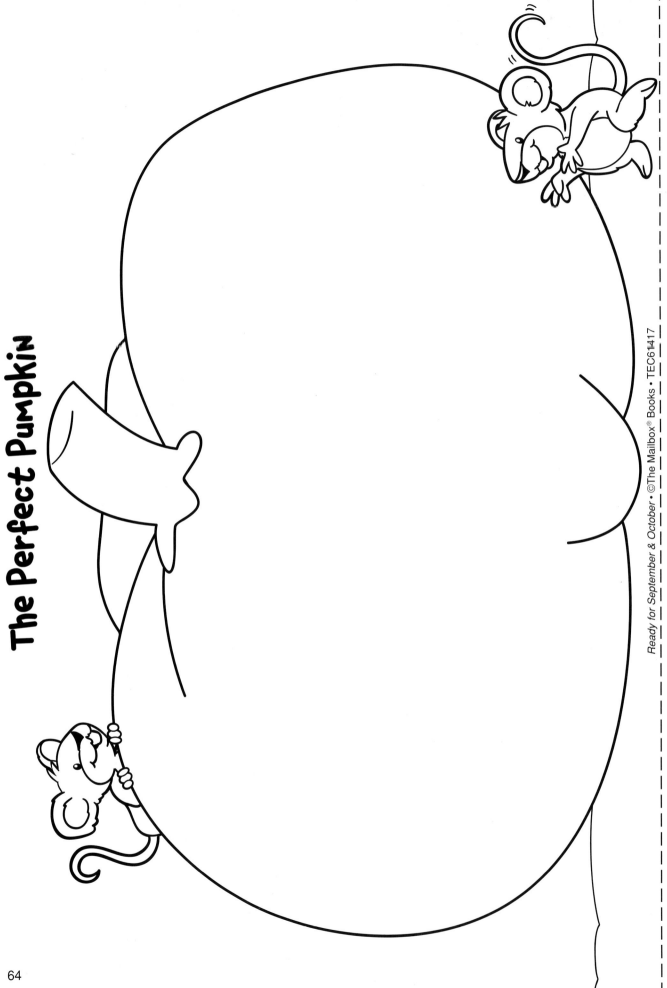

Note to the teacher: Use with "Pumpkin Seed Painting" on page 57.

64

Directions: Cut out the cards below and on page 67. Use them with the mats on pages 69 and 71 for a partner-style lotto game. **For individual use,** provide • one mat and one set of cards to use as a matching activity.

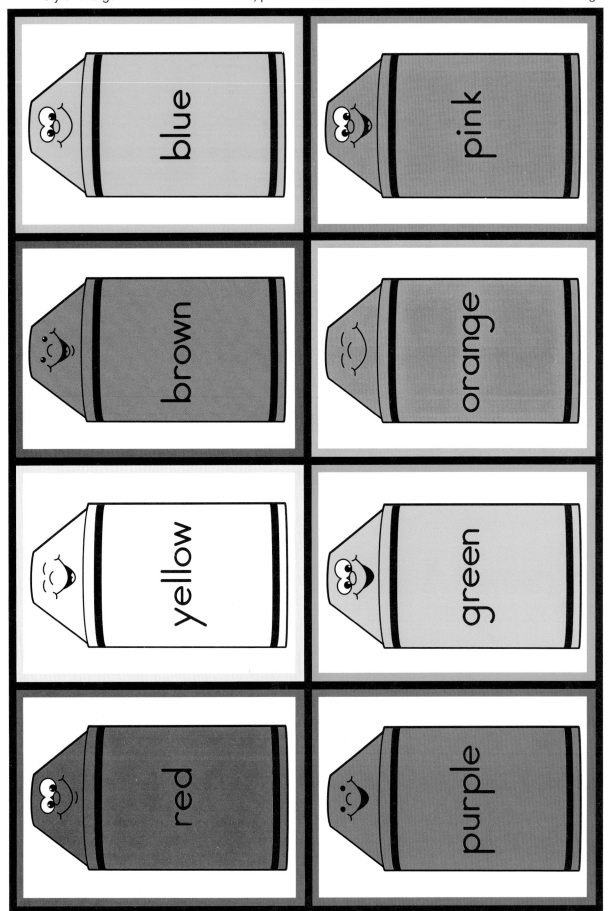

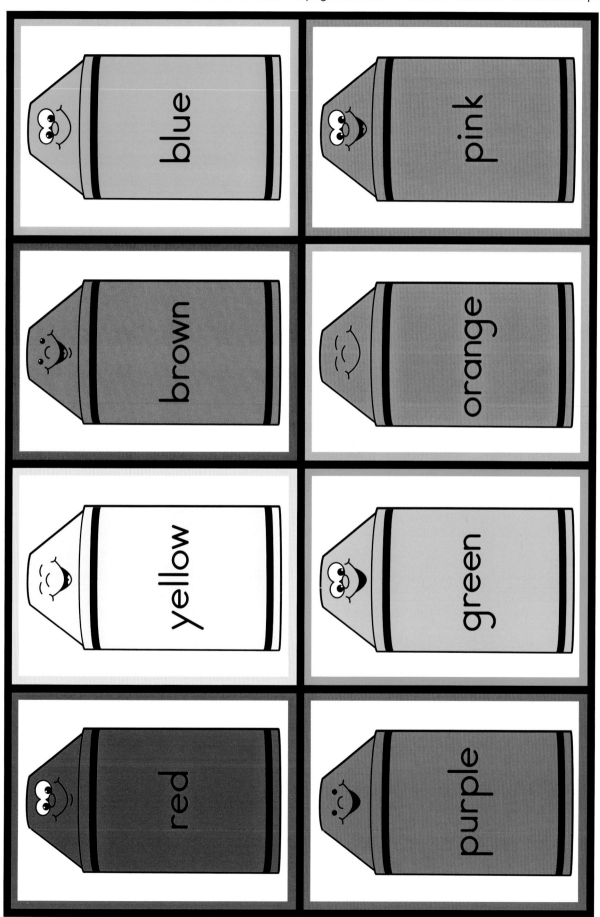

68

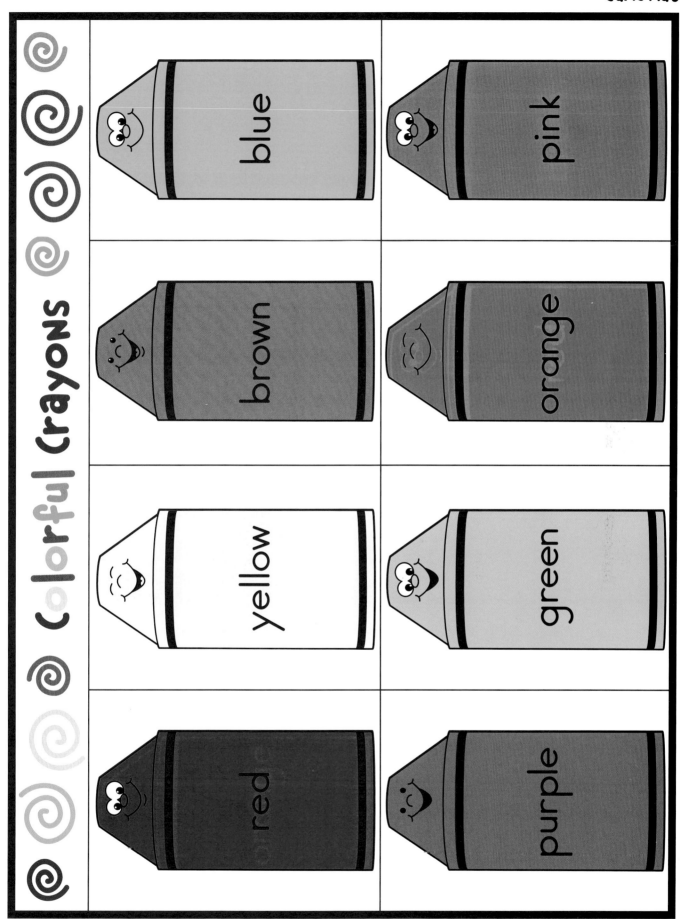

Colorful Crayons

blue

pink

brown

orange

yellow

green

red

purple

Ready for September & October • ©The Mailbox® Books • TEC61417

Math game: Use with the mat on page 71, the directions on page 65, and the cards on pages 65 and 67.

Colorful Crayons
TEC61417

Use with the cards on page 75 for matching games in your pocket chart, Concentration-style partner or small-group games, and individual assessment of letter knowledge.

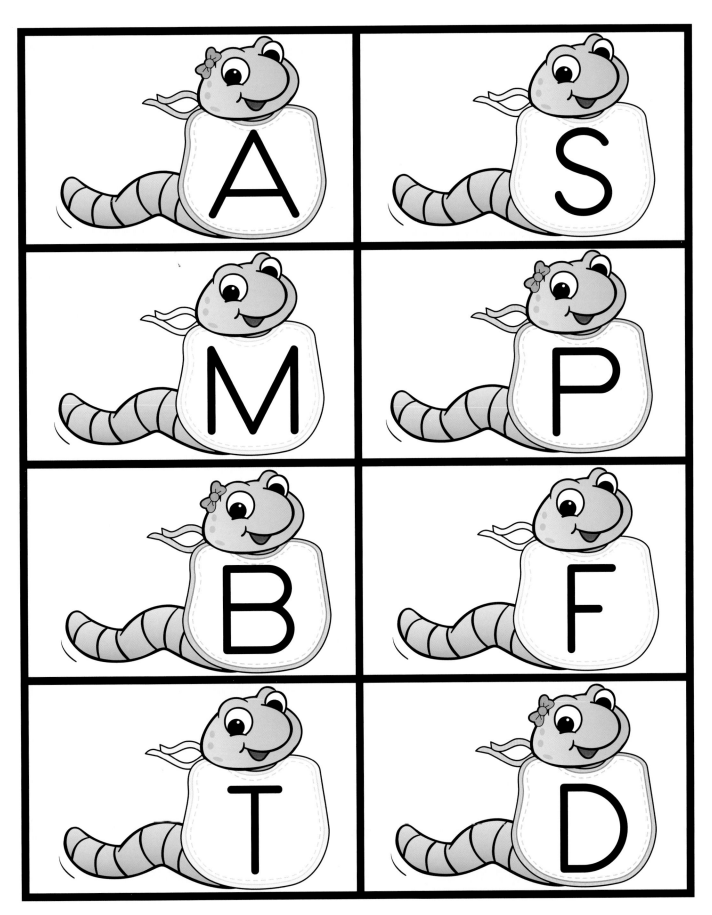

Tell youngsters a brief story about two baskets of apples: One basket fell from its owner's arms, and the apples rolled all the way down a hill, making them very dizzy! When all the apples reached the cider mill, they were mixed together. Have students sort the dizzy apple cards from the ones that did not roll down the hill. Then have students re-sort them by apple color.

Rake and Rhyme

Ready for September & October • ©The Mailbox® Books • TEC61417

Literacy center: Remove this mat and put it in a plastic page protector for durability. Then put the mat and the cards from page 83 at a center. Scatter the cards facedown. A child flips two cards and says the picture words. If the words rhyme, he places the cards on the mat. If not, he turns them back over and repeats the process.

81

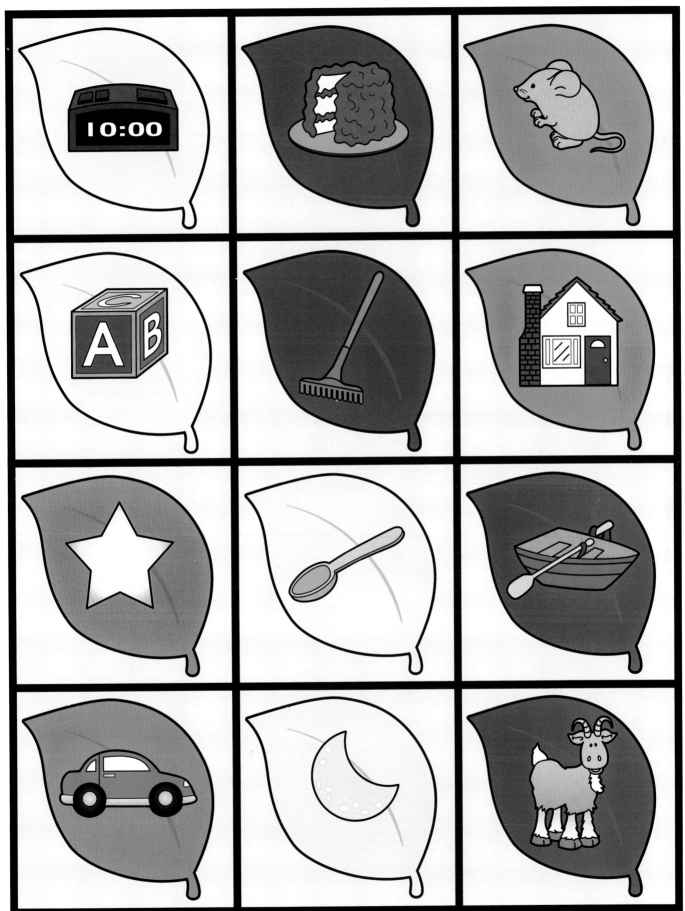

Rake and Rhyme
TEC61417

Rake and Rhyme
TEC61417

Rake and Rhyme
TEC61417

Rake and Rhyme
TEC61417

Rake and Rhyme
TEC61417

Rake and Rhyme
TEC61417

Rake and Rhyme
TEC61417

Rake and Rhyme
TEC61417

Rake and Rhyme
TEC61417

Rake and Rhyme
TEC61417

Rake and Rhyme
TEC61417

Rake and Rhyme
TEC61417

Cut out the cards and use them with the leaf pattern strips on page 87 for center and small-group patterning activities, large-group patterning activities in your pocket chart, and individual assessment of patterning skills. If desired, also use the cards for creating your own *AB* or *ABC* patterns.

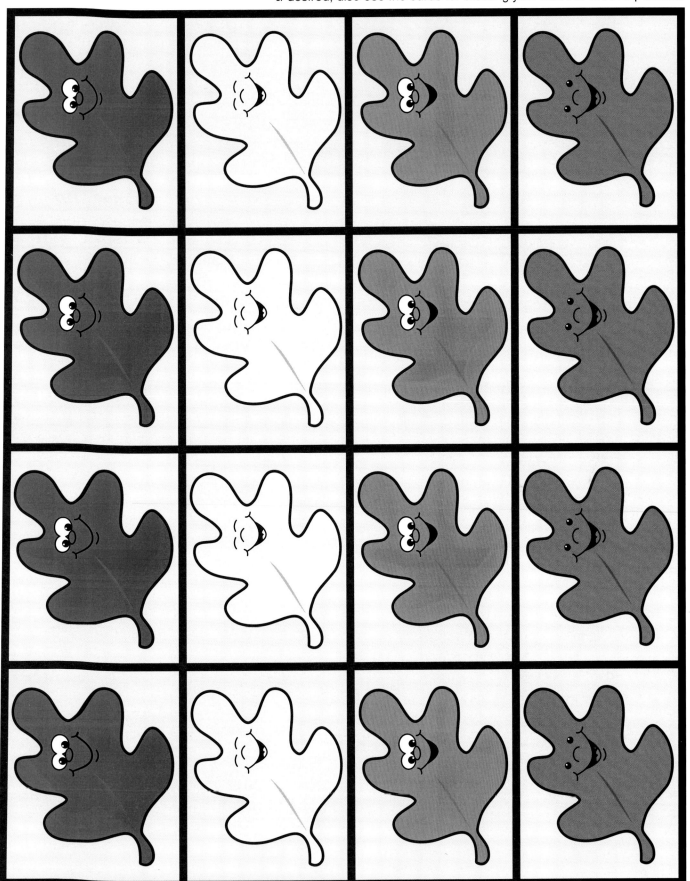

TEC61417

TEC61417

TEC61417

TEC61417

88

Perfect Pumpkin Patch

Ready for September & October • ©The Mailbox® Books • TEC61417

Literacy game: Remove this mat and put it in a plastic page protector for durability. Use with the mat on page 91 and the cards and directions on page 93.

Perfect Pumpkin Patch

TEC61417

Perfect Pumpkin Patch

Ready for September & October • ©The Mailbox® Books • TEC61417

Literacy game: Remove this mat and put it in a plastic page protector for durability. Use with the mat on page 89 and the cards and directions on page 93.

Perfect Pumpkin Patch

TEC61417

Directions for two players:
1. Choose a mat. Spread the cards facedown.
2. When it is your turn, flip a card and say the picture word.
3. If the word begins with /p/, like **pumpkin**, place the card on your mat. If not, turn the card back over.
4. The game ends when all eight beginning sound /p/ cards are on the mats.

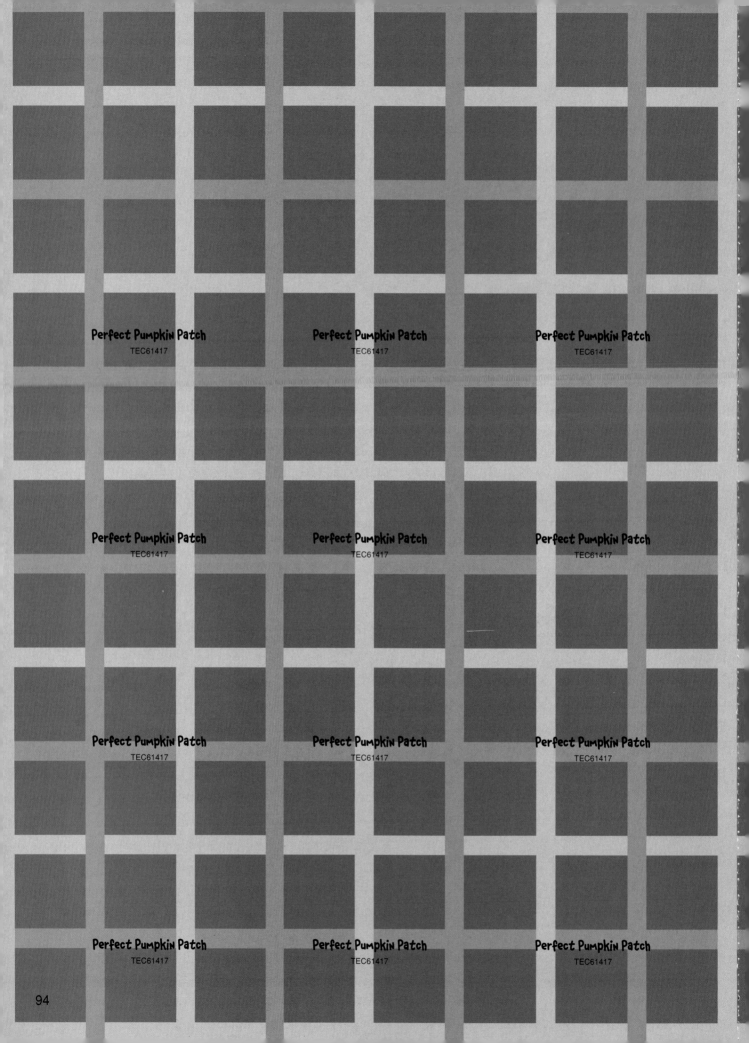

Perfect Pumpkin Patch
TEC61417

Perfect Pumpkin Patch
TEC61417

Perfect Pumpkin Patch
TEC61417

Perfect Pumpkin Patch
TEC61417

Perfect Pumpkin Patch
TEC61417

Perfect Pumpkin Patch
TEC61417

Perfect Pumpkin Patch
TEC61417

Perfect Pumpkin Patch
TEC61417

Perfect Pumpkin Patch
TEC61417

Perfect Pumpkin Patch
TEC61417

Perfect Pumpkin Patch
TEC61417

Perfect Pumpkin Patch
TEC61417

Cut out the cards and place them faceup in random order. A child arranges the cards, in order, to show a cat decorating a pumpkin from start to finish. Then she uses the picture details to tell a story.

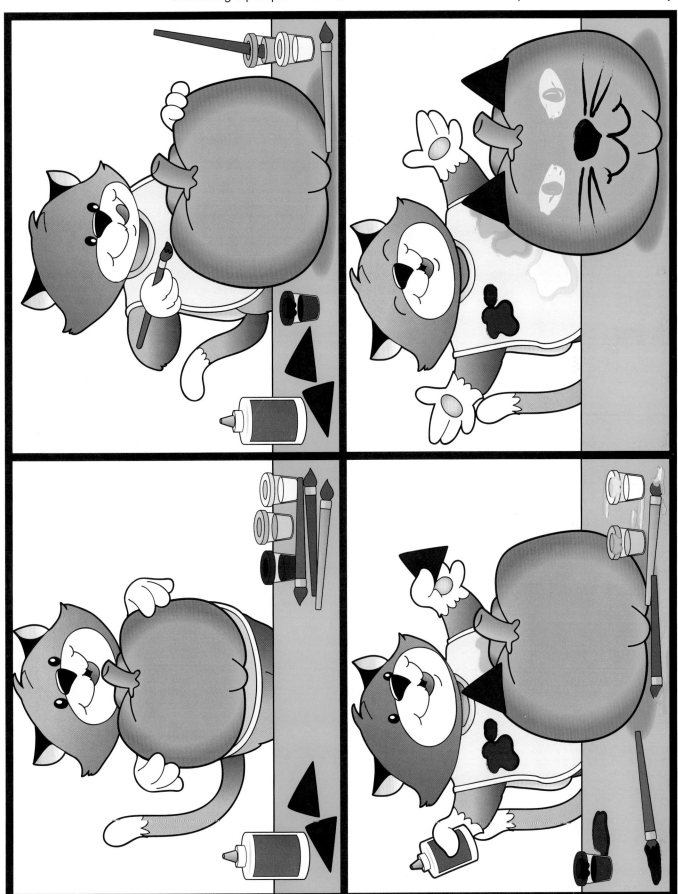